Cocoa & Coco

Who Are We?

By Kakakou

Cocoa: Who am I?
Coco: Who are we?

COCOA
COCO

Cocoa: Let's look around.
Coco: Yes! Let's see.

COCO

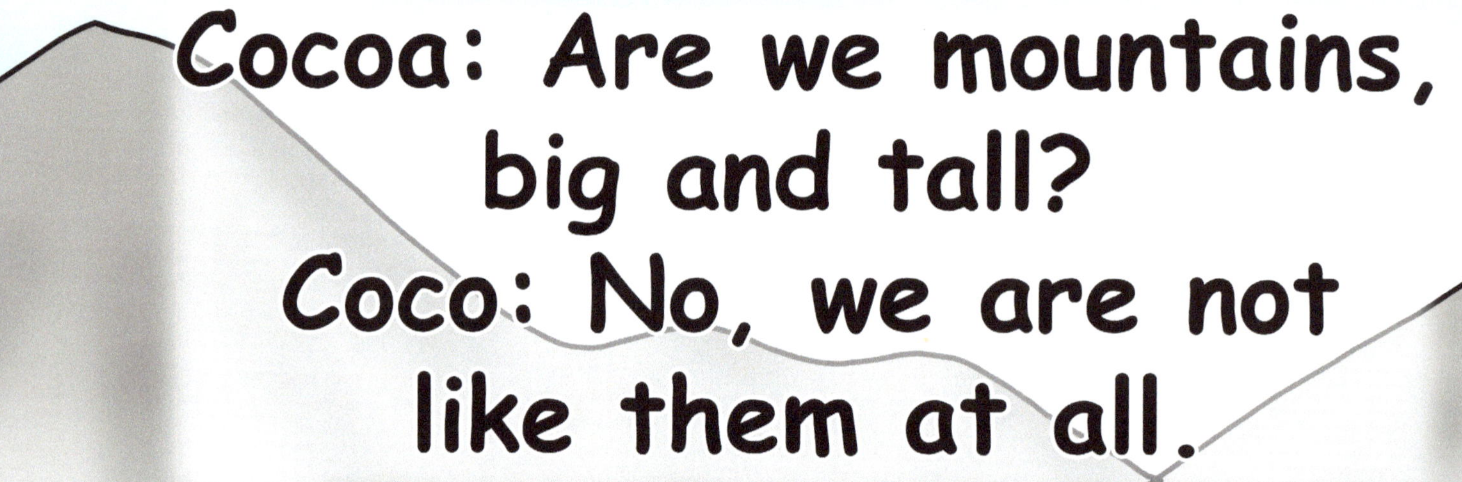

Cocoa: Are we mountains, big and tall?
Coco: No, we are not like them at all.

Cocoa: Are we streams that glisten in the sun?
Coco: No, we do not flow, not even for fun.

Cocoa: Are we trees with leaves and fruits?
Coco: No, we don't have roots or shoots.

Cocoa: Are we flowers, beautiful and bright?
Coco: No, we don't bloom all day and night.

Cocoa: Are we the moon
up high?
Coco: No, we do not live
up in the sky.

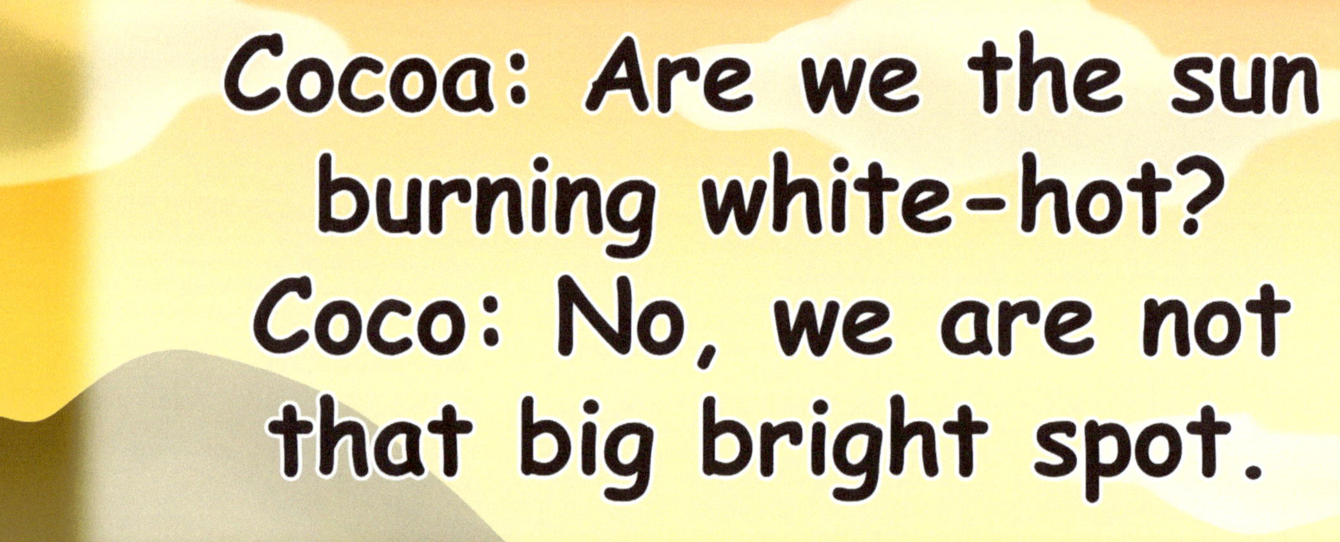

Cocoa: Are we the sun burning white-hot?
Coco: No, we are not that big bright spot.

Cocoa: Are we the sky,
so big and blue?
Coco: No, we do not
have such a vast view.

COCOA
COCO

Coco: Are we bees making honey?
Cocoa: No, we don't buzz around sounding funny.

Coco: Are we birds flapping our wings?
Cocoa: No, we do not tweet in the spring.

Coco: Are we animals that jump and walk?
Cocoa: No, we wear clothes and can talk.

Coco: Then who am I? And who are you?
Cocoa: Relax! I'll show you what's true.

COCO
COCOA

Coco: Please tell me, who are we?
Cocoa: Close your eyes and count 1, 2, 3...

COCO
COCOA

Coco: Look in the mirror.
It's you and me!
Cocoa: We are small
humans; now do you see?

COCO
COCO

Coco: Yes! We are toddlers, but we are not alike.
Cocoa: We are twins. Yes! You got it right.

COCOA
COCOA

Cocoa: Who are you?
Can you tell?
Coco: Yes! I'm a little
boy with curly hair.

COCO

Coco: Who are you? Can you tell?
Cocoa: Yes! I am a little girl with curly hair like you.

COCOA

Cocoa: Yes! I am a little girl with curly hair like you.

COCOA
COCO

Coco: Look around. It's beautiful and sunny.
Cocoa: Over there! The grasshoppers look so funny.

Coco and Cocoa together:
Cocoa and Coco are the
sweetest names.
We love having fun and
playing games.

COCO
COCOA

Coco and Cocoa together
We are twins with
different faces. Together,
we explore many places.

COCOA
CO

Coco: We love each other, and Cocoa is the best sister.
Cocoa: Yes! I am the best sister, and you are the best brother.

COCOA
COX